What Allah says about Spying, Backbiting and Slander!

Do not spy. Do not grope after the secrets of the people. Do not search for their defects and weaknesses. Do not pry into their conditions and affairs. Whether this is done because of suspicion, or for an evil intention to cause harm to somebody, or for satisfying one's own curiosity, in every case it is forbidden by the Shari 'ah. It does not befit a believer that he should spy on the hidden affairs of other people, and should try to peep at them from behind curtains to find out their defects and their weaknesses. This also includes reading other people's private letters, listening secretly to private conversations, peeping into the neighbor's house, and trying to get information in different ways about the domestic life or private affairs of others. This is grave immorality which causes serious mischief in society. That is why the Holy Prophet (saws) once said in an address about those who pry into other people's affairs:
"O people, who have professed belief verbally, but faith has not yet entered your hearts. Do not pry into the affairs of the Muslims,

for he who will pry into the affairs of the Muslims, Allah will pry into his affairs, and he whom Allah investigates will be disgraced by Allah in his own house. " (Abu Da'ud)

In a hadith the Holy Prophet (saws) said; "If you start prying into the secret affairs of the people, you will corrupt them, or at least drive them very near corruption." (Abu Da'ud)

In another Hadith he said: "When you happen to form an evil opinion about somebody, do not pry about it. " (Al-Jassas, Ahkam al-Qur'an)

According to still another Hadith, the Holy Prophet (saws) said: "The one who saw a secret affair of somebody and then concealed it, is as though he saved a girl who had been buried alive." (Al-Jassas)

The unlawfulness of spying is not only applicable to individuals, but also to the Islamic government. The duty, of forbidding the people to do evil, that the Shari`ah (Islamic Law) has entrusted to the government, does not require that it should establish a system of spying, to inquire too curiously into the people's secret evils, and then punish them. However, it should use force against those evils, which are manifested openly. As for the hidden evils, spying is not the way to reform them. It is education, preaching, counseling, collective training of the people and trying to create a pure social environment. In this connection, an incident concerning Umar, when he was the Caliph, is very instructive.

Once, at night, he heard the voice of a person singing in the next house. He became curious and climbed the wall. There he saw wine as well as a woman. He shouted at the man, saying: "O enemy of Suspicion, do you think you will disobey Allah, and Allah will not expose your secret?" The man replied: "Do not make haste, O Commander of the Faithful. If I have committed one sin, you have committed three sins.

Allah has forbidden spying, and you have spied. Allah has commanded that one should enter the houses by the doors, and you have entered my house, by climbing over the wall. Allah has commanded that one should avoid entering the other people's houses without permission, and you have entered my house without my permission." Hearing this reply Umar confessed his error, and did not take any action against the man, but made him promise that he would follow the right way in the future.

This shows that it is not only forbidden for individuals, but also for the Islamic government to pry into the secrets of the people, and discover their sins, and errors and then seize them for punishment. The same thing has been said in a Hadith in which the Holy Prophet (saws) has said: "When the ruler starts searching for the causes of suspicions among the people he corrupts them." (Abu Da'ud)

The only exceptions from this Command are the special cases and situations in which spying is actually needed. For instance, if in the conduct of a person, some signs of corruption are visible, and there is fearfulness that he is about to commit a crime, the government can inquire into his affairs. e.g., If somebody sends a proposal of marriage to the house of a person, or one wants to enter into business with someone, the other person can inquire and investigate into his affairs for his own satisfaction.

Allah says: "O you who have believed, avoid much suspicion, for some suspicions are sins. Do not spy, nor should any one backbite the other. Is there any among you who would like to eat the flesh of his dead brother? Nay, you yourselves despise it. Fear Allah, for Allah is Acceptor of repentance and All-Merciful." [49 Al-Hujuraat: 12]

The lives, property and privacy of all citizens in an Islamic society are considered sacred, whether or not the person is Muslim. Non-Muslims have freedom of worship and the practice of their religions, including their own family law and religious courts. They are obliged to pay a tax (Jizyah) instead of the Zakah, and the state is obligated to provide both protection and government services. Before the modern era, it was extremely rare to find a state or government anywhere in the world that was as careful of its minorities, and their civil rights as the Islamic states.

What Allah says about Backbiting!

Allah says: "Doomed (to ruin) is every such person who slanders others and backbites them habitually." [104 Humazah: 1]

Gheebat (back-biting) has been defined thus: "It is saying behind the back of a person something which would hurt him if he knew of it." This definition has been reported from the Holy Prophet (saws).

According to another tradition related on the authority of Abu Hurairah, the Holy Prophet (saws) defined backbiting as follows: "It is talking about your brother in an irritating way." It was asked: "What, if the defect being talked of is present in the brother?" The Holy Prophet (saws) replied: "If it is present in him, it would be backbiting. If it is not there, it would be slandering him. "

In another tradition which Imam Malik has related in Mu'watta, "A person asked the Holy Prophet: What is backbiting? The Holy Prophet replied: "It is talking of your brother in an irritating way. He then asked: Even if it is true, O Messenger of Allah? He replied: If what you said was false, it would then be defamation."

These traditions make it plain that uttering a false accusation against a person in his absence is defaming while describing a real defect in him is backbiting. Whether this is done in specific words, or by suggestion, in every case it is forbidden. Likewise, whether this is done in the lifetime of a person, or after his death, it is forbidden in both cases.

When a man had been stoned to death for committing adultery, the Holy Prophet (saws) heard a man saying to his companion: "Look at this man. Allah had concealed his secret, but he himself did not leave it alone until he was killed like a dog!" While on their way they saw the dead body of an ass lying rotting. The Holy Prophet (saws) stopped, called the two men and said: "Come down and butcher this dead ass." They asked: "Who will eat it, O Messenger of Allah?" The Holy Prophet (saws) said: "A little before this you were attacking the honor of your brother that was much worse than eating this dead ass."

The only exceptions to this restriction are in cases in which there may be a genuine need to speak of a person "behind his back, or after his death," and if it was not done a greater evil might result than backbiting itself. The Holy Prophet (saws) has described this exception as a judicial principle, thus the Prophet (saws) said: "The worst excess is to attack the honor of a Muslim unjustly." (Abu Da'ud)

In this saying the condition of "unjustly" points out that doing so "in justice" is permissible. Then, in the practice of the Holy Prophet (saws) we find some precedents, which show what is implied by "justice," and in what conditions and cases backbiting may be lawful to the extent necessary.

Two of the Companions, each sent a proposal of marriage to a lady. She came to the Holy Prophet (saws) and asked for his advice. He said: "Mu`awiyah is a poor man and Abu Jahm beats his wives much." (Bukhari, Muslim)

In this case, as there was the question of the lady's future, and she had consulted the Holy Prophet (saws) for his advice, he deemed it necessary to inform her of the two men's weaknesses.

Once Hind bint 'Utbah, wife of Abu Sufyan, came to the Holy Prophet (saws) and said: "Abu Sufyan is a miserly person. He does not provide enough for me and my children's needs. " (Bukhari, Muslim)

Although this complaint from the wife in the absence of the husband was backbiting, the Holy Prophet (saws) permitted it, for the oppressed person has a right that he or she may take the complaint of injustice to a person who has the power to get it removed.

When is Backbiting permissible!

From these and other precedents of the Traditions of the Holy Prophet (saws), the jurists and traditionists have deduced this judicial principle. Backbiting is permissible only in case it is needed for a real and genuine (this means genuine from the Shari'ah point of view) necessity, and the necessity may not be satisfied without having to resort to it. Then on the basis of the same principle the scholars have declared that backbiting is permissible in the following cases:

(1) Complaining by an oppressed person against an oppressor to every person he thinks can do something to save him from injustice.

(2) Mentioning the evils of a person (or persons) with the intention of reforming them.

(3) Stating the facts of a case before a legal expert for the purpose of seeking a religious or legal ruling regarding an unlawful act committed by a person.

(4) Warning the people of the mischiefs of a person (or persons) so that they may ward off evil. e. g. It is not only permissible, but obligatory to mention the imperfections of the reporters, witnesses and writers, for without it, it is not possible to safeguard the Shari ah against the spreading of false reports, or safeguarding the courts against injustices, on the common people, or safeguarding students against errors and misunderstandings. If a person wants to have the relationship

of marriage with somebody, or wishes to rent a house in the neighborhood of somebody, or wants to give something into the custody of somebody for safekeeping, and consults another person, it is obligatory for him to apprise him of all aspects so that he is not deceived because of ignorance.

(5) To raise ones voice against and criticize the evils of the people who may be spreading sin, immorality and error, or corrupting the people's faith, and persecuting them.

(6) To use nicknames for the people who may have become well known by those names, but this should be done for the purpose of recognition, and not with a view to embarass and hurt them.

Apart from these exceptions it is absolutely forbidden to speak ill of a person behind his back. If what is spoken is true, it is backbiting; if it is false, it is defamation; and if it is meant to make two persons quarrel, it is slander. The Shari 'ah has declared all these as forbidden. In the Islamic society, it is incumbent on every Muslim to refute a false charge made against a person in his presence, and not to listen to it quietly, and not tell those who are speaking ill of somebody, without a genuine religious need, to desist from the sin.

The Holy Prophet (saws) has said: If a person does not support and help a Muslim when he is being disgraced, and his honor is being attacked, Allah also does not support and help him when he stands in need of Allah's help. If a person helps and supports a Muslim, when his honor is being attacked, and he is being disgraced, Allah Almighty also helps him when he wants that Allah should help him. (Abu Da'ud)

As for the backbiter, as soon as he realizes that he is committing this sin, or has committed it, his first duty is to offer repentance before Allah, and restrain himself from this forbidden act. His second duty is that he should compensate for it as far as possible. If he has backbitten a dead person, he should ask Allah's forgiveness for the person as often as he can. If he has backbitten a living person, and what he said was also false, he should refute it before the people before whom he had made the defamation.

If what he said was true, he should never speak ill of him in the future, and should ask for the pardon of the person whom he had backbitten. A section of scholars are of the opinion that pardon should be asked only in case the other person has come to know of it; otherwise one should only offer repentance. If the person concerned is unaware of the backbiter, and he goes and tells him that he had backbitten him, he would certainly feel hurt.

Allah, by likening backbiting to eating a dead brother's flesh, has given the idea of its being a shame. Eating the flesh of the dead is by itself detestable. When the flesh is not of an animal, but of a man, and of one's own dead brother, abomination would be added to shame. Then, by presenting the comparison in the cross-examination tone of voice, it has been made more impressive, so that every person may ask his own conscience, and decide whether he would like to eat the flesh of his dead brother. If he would not, and he despises it by nature, how would he like it if his honor was attacked by his brother-in-faith in his absence, when he cannot defend himself, and when he is unaware that he is being disgraced.

This shows that the basic reason for forbidding backbiting is not that the person being backbitten is being hurt, but speaking ill of a person in his absence is by itself unlawful and forbidden, whether he is aware of it, or not, and whether he feels hurt by it or not. Obviously, eating the flesh of a dead man is not forbidden because it hurts the dead man. The dead person is totally unaware that somebody is eating from his body, but because this act by itself is a horror.

Likewise, if the person who is backbitten also does not come to know of it through any means, he will remain unaware throughout his life that somebody had attacked his honor, at a particular time before some particular people, and on that account he had stood disgraced in the eyes of those people. Because of his unawareness, he will not feel at all hurt by this backbiting, but his honor would in any case be disgraced. Therefore, this act in its nature is not any different from eating the flesh of a dead brother.

Lessons to be learned from the slandering of A'ishah!

Allah says: "Those who have invented the slander, are some of your own people. You should not, however, regard this matter as evil, for it has good in it for you. Whosoever took any part in this, he earned his share of the sin accordingly, and the one, who had the greatest share of responsibility in it, shall have a terrible punishment. When you heard of it, why didn't the Believing men and Believing women have a good opinion of themselves, and why did they not say, "This is a clear slander?" Why did the slanderers not bring four witnesses (to prove their charge)? Now that they have not brought witnesses, they themselves are liars in the sight of Allah. Were it not for Allah's grace and mercy towards you in this world, and in the Hereafter, a painful scourge would have visited you because of the things, which you were involved in. (Just think, how erroneous you were) when you passed this lie on from one tongue to the other, and uttered with your mouths that of which you had no knowledge. You took it as a trifling matter whereas it was a grave offense in the sight of Allah." [24 An-Noor:11-15]

This verse is a reference to the slander against A'ishah. Allah, Himself, has described it as a false accusation, and slander, which implies its total denial. From here begins mention of the incident, which provided the occasion of this Chapter's revelation. We have reproduced the initial part of it in the Introduction as related by A' ishah herself. The rest of it is reproduced below. A'ishah says:

"Rumors about this slander went on spreading in the city for about a month, which caused great distress and anguish to the Holy Prophet (saws). I cried, due to helplessness, and my parents were sick with mental agony. At last one day the Holy Prophet (saws) visited us. He sat near me, which he had not done since the slander had begun. Feeling that something decisive was going to happen that day, Abu Bakr and Umm Ruman (A'ishah's father and mother) also sat near us. The Holy Prophet (saws) started the conversation, saying: A'ishah. I have heard this and that about you. If you are innocent, I expect that Allah will declare your innocence. However, if you have committed a sin, you should offer repentance, and ask for Allah's forgiveness. When a servant (of Allah) confesses his guilt and repents, Allah forgives him.

Hearing these words, tears dried in my eyes. I looked up to my father expecting that he would reply to the Holy Prophet (saws), but he said, daughter, I do not know what I should say. Then I turned to my mother, but she also did not know what to say. At last I said, You have all heard something about me, and believed it. Now, if I say that I am innocent, and Allah is my witness that I am innocent, you will not believe me. If I confess something which I never did, and Allah knows that I never did it, you will believe me. At that time I tried to call to memory the name of Prophet Jacob, but could not recall it. Therefore, in view of the predicament that I was placed in, I said, I cannot, but repeat the words, which the father of Prophet Joseph had spoken.

I will bear this patiently with good grace. Saying this I lay down, and turned to the other side. I was thinking that Allah was aware of my innocence, and He would certainly reveal the truth, but I could never imagine that Divine Revelation would come down in my defense, which the people will read and recite until the Last Day. What I thought was, the Holy Prophet (saws) would see in a dream in which Allah would indicate my innocence. But in the meantime suddenly, the state of receiving Revelation appeared on the Holy Prophet (saws), when pearl like drops of perspiration used to gather on his face, even in winter. We all held our breath and sat silent. As for me I was fearless, but my parents seemed to be struck with fear. They did not know what the Divine Revelation would be.

When the Revelation was over, the Holy Prophet (saws) seemed to be very pleased. Overjoyed with happiness the words he spoke were: Congratulations A'ishah, Allah has sent down proof of your innocence, and then he recited these ten verses (11-21 of Chapter an-Noor). At this my mother said to me, Get up and thank the Holy Prophet (saws). I said, I shall neither thank him nor, you two, but thank Allah Who has sent down my absolution. You did not even so much as contradict the charge against me.

One point to be understood here is that before mentioning the absolution of A'ishah, a full section of verses has been devoted to the Commands pertaining to zina, which Allah admonishes is not a slight matter, which may be used as a means of entertaining the people in a gathering. It is very serious. If the accuser is right in his accusation he should produce witnesses, and get a most horrible punishment inflicted upon the adulterer, and the adulteress. If the accuser is false, he deserves to be given 80 lashes, so that nobody may dare to bring a false charge against another person.

If the accuser is a husband, he will have to bring charges in a court of law to settle the matter. So, none who speaks such an accusation will have peace. The Islamic society, which has been brought about for the purpose of establishing goodness, and piety in the world, can neither tolerate zina, as a means of entertainment, nor endure loose talk about it as a diversion and amusement.

Only a few persons have been mentioned in traditions, who were spreading the rumors. They were hypocrites. The other Muslims, who had been involved in the mischief was due to misunderstanding, and weakness. The other people who were more or less involved have not been mentioned in the books of Hadith and life of the Holy Prophet (saws). Though the hypocrites, according to their own presumptions, made the worst attack, it brought misfortune on them, and proved to be a blessing in disguise for the Holy Prophet (saws).

As mentioned in the Introduction, the hypocrites had planned to inflict a defeat on the Muslims, on the moral front, which was their real field of superiority, and was responsible for their victory on every other front against their opponents. However, Allah turned this mischief into a means of strength for the Muslims. On this occasion, the conduct and attitude adopted by the Holy Prophet (saws), his family, and the Muslims at large proved beyond any doubt that they were the purest people, morally tolerant, and just in nature, as well as, noble and forbearing in character. If the Holy Prophet (saws) had wished, he could have gotten the people responsible for the attack on his honor, beheaded immediately. But he bore everything with patience for a whole month.

Then, when a Divine ruling came down from Allah, he enforced the punishment only on those three Muslims whose guilt was established. He even spared the hypocrites. Abu Bakr's own relative, whose whole family he had been supporting, continued heaping disgrace on him publicly. However, that noble man neither severed his family relations with him, nor stopped monetary help to him, and his family. None of the wives of the Holy Prophet (saws) took the least part in the slander, nor even expressed the slightest approval of it. So much so that Zainab (a wife of the Holy Prophet (saws), whose real sister was taking part in the slander, did not utter anything about her rival (A'ishah) except good words. According to A'ishah, herself: "Zainab, among the wives of the Holy Prophet (saws) was my strongest rival, but when in connection with the incident of the slander, the Holy Prophet (saws) asked her opinion of me, she said, `O Messenger of Allah, I swear by Allah that I have perceived nothing in her except piety."

A'ishah's own nobility of character can be judged by this that though Hassan bin Thabit had played a prominent role in the campaign of slander against her, she continued to treat him with due honor and esteem. When the people reminded her that he was the man who had slandered her, she retorted, no, he it was, who used to rebut the anti-Islamic poets on behalf of the Holy Prophet (saws), and Islam. Such was the conduct and attitude of those people who were directly affected by the slander. As for the other Muslims, their attitude can be judged from one instance.

When Abu Ayyub Ansari's wife mentioned to him the rumors of the slander, he said, "Mother of Ayyub, if you had been there in place of A'ishah, would you have done that?" She replied, "By Allah, I would never have done it." Ayyub then said, "Well, A'ishah is a much better woman than you. As for myself, if I had been in the place of Safwan, I could never have entertained such an evil thought, and Safwan is a better Muslim than I. Thus, the result of the mischief engineered by the hypocrites was contrary to what they had planned to achieve, and the Muslims emerged out of this test morally stronger than before.

There was more good to come from this. The incident became the cause of some very important additions to the social law, and rulings of Islam. Through these rulings the Muslims received such Commandments from Allah by which the Muslim society can be kept clean, and protected against the creation and propagation of moral evils, and if they arise at all, they can be corrected promptly.

Furthermore, there was another aspect of goodness in it also. The Muslims came to understand fully that the Holy Prophet (saws) had no knowledge of the unseen. He knew only that which Allah taught him. Besides that, his knowledge was the same as that of a common man. For one full month he remained in great anxiety with regard to A'ishah. He would sometimes make enquiries from the maid-servant, sometimes from his other wives.

At last when he spoke to A'ishah, he spoke only this: "If you have committed the sin, you should offer repentance, and if you are innocent, I expect that Allah will declare your innocence." Had he possessed any knowledge of the unseen, he would not have felt so upset, nor would he have made enquiries, nor counselled her on repentance. However, when a Divine Message revealed the truth, he received that knowledge, which he had not possessed for more than a month.

Thus, Allah arranged to safeguard the Muslims, through direct experience and observation, against exaggerated notions, which people generally get involved in regarding their religious leaders, on account of excessive blind faith. Perhaps this was the reason why Allah withheld Revelation for a month, for if Revelation had been sent down on the day of the false accusation, it could not have had any beneficial effect.

This may also be translated as: "Why did they not have a good opinion of the people of their own community and society?" The words in the Text are comprehensive and contain a subtle meaning which should be understood well. What happened concerning A'ishah and Safwan bin Mu`attal was only this: A woman, belonging to the caravan was left behind. A man belonging to the same caravan was also left behind. He saw her and brought her on his camel to the camp.

Now if a person alleges that when the two found themselves alone, they became involved in sin, the accusation would imply two other hypotheses:

> First, if the accuser himself (whether man or woman) had been there, he would certainly have availed of the rare opportunity and committed the sinful act, for he had never before chanced upon a person of the opposite sex in a situation like this.
>
> Second, the accuser's assessment of the moral condition of the society he belongs to is that in that society there is no

man or woman who could possibly have abstained from sin in similar circumstances. This will be the case when it involves any man, and any woman.

However, suppose if the man and woman happened to belong to the same place, and the woman who was left behind by chance was the wife, sister, or daughter of a friend, relative, neighbor, or an acquaintance of the man, the matter would become much more serious and grave. Then it would mean that the one who utters such an accusation has a very poor and degraded opinion of himself, as well as of his society, which has nothing to do with morality and good sense. No gentleman can imagine that if he finds a woman belonging to the family of a friend, a neighbor, or an acquaintance, stranded on the way, the first thing he would do, would be to molest and dishonor her, and then think of escorting her home.

Here the matter was a thousand times more serious. The lady was no other than the wife of the Holy Prophet of Allah (saws), whom every Muslim esteemed higher than his own mother, and whom Allah, Himself, had forbidden for every Muslim just like his own mother. The man was not only a follower of the same caravan, a soldier of the same army, an inhabitant of the same city, but also a Muslim, who believed the lady's husband to be the Messenger of Allah. He was his religious leader and guide, and had even followed him, and fought in the most dangerous battle at Badr. Viewed against this background, it would seem that the person who uttered such an accusation, and those who considered the accusation as probable, formed a very poor opinion, not only of their moral selves, but also of the whole society.

That means, the accusation was not worthy of any consideration. The Muslims should have rejected it there and then as a lie, and a falsehood. A question might be asked: Why did the Holy Prophet (saws) and Abu Bakr Siddiq not reject it on the very same day, and why did they give it all that importance? The answer is that the position of the husband and the father is different from that of the common people. Though none else can know a woman better than her husband, and a righteous husband cannot doubt the character of a virtuous, and pious wife only on account of the people's accusations, but when the wife is accused, the husband is placed in a difficult situation. Even if he rejects it outright as a lie, the accusers will not listen. They will rather say that the woman is clever, and has fooled the husband into believing that she is virtuous and pious, whereas she is not.

A similar situation is faced by the parents. They also cannot remove the accusers slander, regarding their daughter's chastity, even if they know that the accusation is false. The same thing had afflicted the Holy Prophet (saws), Abu Bakr and Umm Ruman, otherwise they did not entertain any doubt about A'ishah's character. That is why the Holy Prophet (saws) declared in his sermon, that he had neither seen any evil in his wife, nor in the man who was being mentioned in the slander.

` .... in the sight of Allah" means in the Law of Allah, or according to the Law of Allah. In Allah's knowledge, the accusation was false, and its falsehood was not dependent on the production of witnesses by the accusers.

Here, nobody should have the misunderstanding that failure to bring witnesses is being regarded as the basis to prove that the accusation was false. This misunderstanding can arise if one does not keep in view the background of the incident. None of the accusers had witnessed the thing, which they were uttering with their tongues. The only basis of their accusation was that A'ishah had been left behind from the caravan, and afterwards Safwan had brought her to the camp on his camel. From this nobody with common sense could conclude that A'ishah's being left behind was intentional.

These are not the ways of those who do these type of things. It cannot happen that the wife of the army commander quietly stays back with a man, and then the same man makes her ride on his camel, and makes haste to catch up with the army at the next stopping place in open daylight, at noon. The situation itself warranted that they were thought to be innocent. There could, however, be some justification of the charge if the accusers had seen something with their own eyes, otherwise the circumstances, on which the accusers had based their accusation, did not contain any ground for doubt, or suspicion.

These verses, especially verse 12, wherein Allah says: "Why didn't the Believing men and the Believing women have a good opinion of themselves," and provide the principle that all dealings in Islamic society must be based on `good faith'. The question of a bad opinion should arise only when there is a definite, and concrete basis for it. Every person should, as a matter of principle, be considered innocent unless there are sound reasons to hold him guilty or suspect. Every person should be considered as truthful unless there are strong grounds for holding him as unreliable.

Allah says: "Why did you not, as soon as you heard of it, say, "It is not proper for us to say such a thing? Glory be to Allah! This is a great slander." Allah warns you that in the future you should never repeat a thing like this, if you are true Believers. Allah makes His Revelations clear to you, and He is All-Knowing, All-Wise." [24 An-Noor:16-18]

Allah says: "As for those, who like that indecency should spread among the Believers, deserve a painful punishment in this world, and in the Hereafter, for Allah knows and you do not know (its consequences). If Allah had not shown His grace and mercy to you, (this scandal would have produced very evil results) Allah is indeed very Kind and Merciful." [24 An-Noor:19-20]

The direct interpretation of the verse, in the context in which it occurs, is this: "Those who propagate evil, publicize it and bring Islamic morality into disrepute, deserve punishment." The words in the text, however, comprehend all the various forms that can be employed for the propagation of evil. These include actual setting up of brothels, production of erotic stories, songs, paintings, plays and dramas as well as all kinds of mixed gatherings at clubs and hotels, which induce the people to immoralities.

The Qur'an holds all those who resort to such things as criminals, who deserve punishment not only in the Hereafter, but in this world as well. Accordingly, it is the duty of Islam to put an end to all means of propagating immorality. Its laws must hold all those acts as distinct offenses, which the Qur'an mentions as crimes against public morality, and declares the offenders punishable.

"You do not know...": "You do not visualize the full impact of individual acts on society as a whole. Allah knows best, the number of people, who are affected by these acts, and their cumulative effect on the collective life of the community. You should trust in Him, and do all you can to eradicate, and suppress the evils pointed out by Him. These are not trivial matters to be treated lightly. They have very serious repercussions, and the offenders must be dealt with severely."

Allah says: "O Believers, do not follow in Satan's footsteps, for he will incite to indecency and wickedness any who follow him. If Allah had not shown His Support and mercy to you, none of you would have been able to cleanse yourself. It is Allah alone Who cleanses, whom He wills, and Allah is All-Hearing, All-Knowing." [24 An-Noor:21]

Satan, is bent upon involving you in all kinds of pollutions and indecencies. Had it not been for the mercy and kindness of Allah Who enables you to differentiate between good, and evil, helps you to educate, and reform yourselves, you would not have been able to lead a pure and virtuous life on the strength of your own faculties, and initiative alone.

It is Allah's Will alone, which decides whom to make pious and virtuous. His decisions are not arbitrary, but based on knowledge. He alone knows who is anxious to live a life of virtue, and who is attracted towards a life of sin. Allah hears a person's most secret talk, and is aware of everything that passes in his mind. It is on the basis of this direct knowledge that Allah decides whom to bless with piety and virtue, and whom to ignore.

Allah says: "Those among you, who are bountiful, persons of means, should not swear on oath that they would withhold their help from their relatives, the indigent and those who have left their homes for the cause of Allah. They should forgive and forbear. Do you not wish that Allah should forgive you? Allah is Forgiving and Merciful." [24 An-Noor:22]

A'ishah stated that after the revelation of verses 11-21 absolving her from the accusation, Abu Bakr swore that he would no longer support his relative. This was because the man had shown absolutely no regard for the relationship, nor for the favors that Abu Bakr had been showing him and his family. At this verse 22 was revealed and Abu Bakr, on hearing it, immediately said: "By Allah! we want that Allah should forgive us."

Consequently, he again started to help his relative, and in a more liberal manner than before. Besides Abu Bakr, some other Companions, who had also sworn that they would discontinue helping those who had taken an active part in the slander. After the revelation of this verse, all of them revoked their oaths, and the ill will that had been created by the mischief was gone.

Here a question may arise as to whether a person, who swears for something and later on revokes the oath on finding that there was no good in it, and adopts a better, more virtuous course, should offer penance for breaking the oath or not. One group of jurists is of the opinion that adoption of the virtuous course itself is the penance, and nothing more needs to be done. They base their argument on this verse where Allah commands Abu Bakr to revoke his oath, but did not require him to atone for it. They also cite a Tradition of the Holy Prophet (saws) in support of their argument, saying: "If anybody takes an oath for something, and later on finds that another course is better and adopts it, his adoption of a better course by itself is the atonement for breaking the oath."

The other group is of the view that there is a clear Commandment in the Qur'an concerning the breaking of oath (2 Al-Baqarah: 225, 5 Al-Maidah: 89), Allah says: "Allah does not take you to task for the oaths you utter vainly, but He will certainly take you to task for the oaths you have sworn in earnest. The penance (for breaking such oaths) is either to feed ten needy persons with more or less the same food as you give to your families, or to clothe them, or to set free from bondage the neck of one man, and he who does not find the means shall fast for three days. This shall be the expiation for your oaths whenever you have sworn (and broken them.) But do keep your oaths. Thus, does Allah make clear to you His commandments. Maybe, you will be grateful." [5 Al-Maidah: 89] This refers to oaths which one utters either through habit, or without any intent and purpose. The breach of such vows neither entails penance, nor makes man liable to Allah's disgrace.

Therefore the earlier Commandment stands. No doubt, Allah commanded Abu Bakr to revoke his oath, but He did not tell him that penance was not necessary. As regards the Tradition of the Holy Prophet (saws), it only means this that the sin of taking an oath for a wrong thing is wiped out when the right course is adopted. It does not absolve one from making penance for the oath itself. Another Tradition of the Holy Prophet (saws) clarifies this view. He said: "Whoso swears for something and then finds that another course is better than the one he had sworn for, he should adopt the better course and atone for his oath." This shows that penance for breaking one's oath and penance of the sin for not doing good are different things. The penance for the sexual intercourse is to adopt the right course, and for the second the same as has been laid down in the Qur'an.

Allah says: "Those who charge with slander Believing women, who are chaste, but simple souls, are accursed in this world and in the Hereafter. There is a great punishment for them. They should not forget the Day when their own tongues and their own hands will bear testimony in regard to their misdeeds. On that Day Allah will give them the full recompense they deserve, and they will realize that Allah is the very Truth, Who makes the Truth manifest." [24 An-Noor:23-25]

The word ghafilat as used in the Text means the women who are simple, unpretentious souls, who do not know any hoax, who have pious hearts, and no idea of immorality. They cannot even imagine that their names could ever be associated with any slander. The Holy Prophet (saws) has said: "To slander chaste women is one of the seven 'deadly' sins." According to another

Tradition, the Holy Prophet (saws) said: "To slander a pious woman suffices to ruin the good deeds of a hundred years."

Allah says: "Impure women are for impure men and impure men for impure women, and pure women are for pure men and pure men for pure women. They are free from those scandals which the slanderers utter. There is forgiveness for them and honorable provision." [24 An-Noor:26]

This verse enunciates a fundamental principle. Impure men are a fit match for impure women and pious men are a fit match for pious women. It never happens that a man is good in all other aspects, but is addicted to a solitary vice. As a matter of fact, his habits, manners and demeanor, all contain a number of evil traits, which sustain and nourish that single vice. It is impossible that a man develops a vice all of a sudden without having any trace of its existence in his demeanor and way of life. This is a psychological truth which everybody experiences in the daily lives of the people.

How is it possible that a man who has lived a pure and morally clean life, will put up with and continue to live for years in love with a wife who is adulterous? Can a woman be imagined, who is an adulteress, but she does not show her evil character through her talk, gait, manners and deportment? Is it possible for a virtuous man of high character to live happily with a woman of this type?

What is being suggested here is that people should not put their belief in any rumor that reaches them. They should carefully see who is being accused, on what account, and whether the accusation fairly sticks to the person or not. When there exists no trace of evidence to support the accusation, people cannot believe it just because a foolish, or wicked person has uttered it.

Some commentators have interpreted this verse to mean that evil things are for the evil people, and good things for the good people. The good people are free from the evil things, which the wicked people utter about them. Some others have interpreted it to mean that evil deeds only go with evil people, and good deeds with good people. Pious people are free from the evil deeds, which the wicked people ascribe to them. Still others interpret it to mean that evil and filthy talk is indulged in only by the evil and filthy people, and good and pious talk only by the good and pious people. Pious people are free from the sort of talk that the mischievous people are indulging in. The words of the verse are comprehensive, and can be interpreted in any of three ways, but the meaning that strikes the reader is the one that we have adopted above, and the same fits in more meaningfully with the context than others.

Allah says: "O Believers, do not enter houses, other than your own, until you have the approval of the inmates and have wished them peace. This is the best way for you. It is expected that you will observe it. Then, if you do not find anyone therein, do not enter until you have been given permission, and if you are told to go back, you should go back. This is a purer way for you, and Allah has full knowledge of what you do. There is, however, no harm if you enter houses, which are not dwelling places, but contain something useful for you. Allah knows what you disclose and what you conceal." [24 An-Noor:27-29]

The Commandments given in the beginning of the Chapter were meant to help destroy evil when it appears in society. The Commandments being given now are meant to prevent the birth of evil, to reform society, and root out the causes responsible for the creation and spread of evil. Before we study these Commandments, it will be useful to understand two things clearly:

The revelation of these Commandments immediately after the Divine appraisal of the incident of the "slander" clearly indicates that permeation of a lie against the noble person of a wife of the Holy Prophet (saws) in the society, was the direct result of the existence of a sexually charged atmosphere. In the sight of Allah there was no other way of cleansing society of the evil:

* than by prohibiting free entry into other people's houses,
* discouraging free mixing of the sexes together,
* forbidding women to appear in their make up before men, excepting a small circle of close relatives,
* banning prostitution,
* exhorting men and women not to remain unmarried for long, and
* arranging marriages even of the slaves and slave-girls.

In other words, the movement of the women without a separating covering, and the presence of a large number of unmarried persons in society were, in the knowledge of Allah, the real causes that gradually give rise to sensuality in society. It was this sexually charged atmosphere, which kept the ears, eyes, tongues and hearts of the people ever ready to get involved in any real or fictitious scandal. Allah in His wisdom did not regard any other measure more suitable and effective than these Commandments to destroy this evil. Otherwise, He would have commanded some other Commandments.

The second important thing to remember is that Divine Law does not merely forbid an evil, or only prescribe a punishment for the offender, but it also puts an end to all those factors, which provide occasions for the evil, or incite, or force a person to commit it. It also imposes curbs on the causes, incentives and means leading to the evil, so as to check the wrongdoer, much before he actually commits the crime. It does not like, that people should freely approach, and loiter near the border lines of sin, and get caught, and punished all the time. It does not merely act as a prosecutor, but as a guide, reformer and helper, too. So it uses all kinds of moral, social and educational devices to help the people safeguard themselves against evil, and vice.

Right of Privacy in Islam!

According to the Arab custom of the pre-Islamic days, people would enter each other's house freely, without permission just by pronouncing good morning, or good evening. This unannounced entry sometimes violated the privacy of the people, and their women folk. Allah enjoined the principle that everybody has a right to privacy, in his own house, and no one is entitled to force his entry unannounced, and without permission of the inmates. The rules and regulations enforced by the Holy Prophet (saws) in society on receipt of the above Commandment are given below:

(1) The 'right of privacy' was not merely confined to the question of entry in the houses, but it was declared as a common right according to which it is forbidden to peep into a house, glance from outside, or even read the other person's letter without his permission. According to Thauban, who was a freed slave of the Holy Prophet (saws), the Holy Prophet (saws) said: "When you have already cast a look into a house, what is then the sense in seeking permission for entry?" (Abu Da`ud)

It has been reported that a man came to see the Holy Prophet (saws) and sought permission for entry while standing just in front of the door. The Holy Prophet (saws) said to him: "Stand aside. The object of the Commandment for seeking permission is to prevent casting of looks inside the house." (Abu Da'ud) The practice of the Holy Prophet (saws) was that whenever he went to see somebody, he would stand aside, to the right or the left of the door, and seek permission as it was not then usual to hang curtains on the doors. (Abu Da'ud) Anas, the attendant of the Holy Prophet (saws), states that a man glanced into the room of the Holy Prophet (saws) from outside. The Holy Prophet (saws) at that time was holding an arrow in his hand. He advanced towards the man in a way as if he would thrust the arrow into his belly. (Abu Da'ud)

According to a tradition, the Holy Prophet (saws) said: "Whoever glances through the letter of his brother without his permission, glances into fire." (Abu Da'ud)

According to Muslim and Bukhari, the Holy Prophet (saws) is reported to have said: "If someone peeps into your house, it will be no sin if you injure his eye with a piece of stone." In another Tradition, he has said: "The inmates of a house, who injure the eye of the man peeping into their house, are not liable to any punishment." Imam Shafi`i has taken this Commandment literally and permits smashing of the eye of the one who casts a glance like this. The Hanafis, however, do not take the Command in the literal sense. They express the opinion that it is applicable only in that case where an outsider forces entry into a house in spite of resistance from the inmates, and has his eye or some other limb smashed in the scuffle. In such a case, no penalty will lie on the inmates.

(2) The jurists have included `hearing' also under `glancing'. For instance, if a blind man enters a house without permission, he will not be able to see anybody, but he will certainly be able to hear whatever is going on in the house. This also amounts to violation of the other person's right of privacy.

(3) The Command to seek permission is not only applicable in cases where a person wants to enter the other people's houses, but it also applies to entry in the house of one's own mother or sister. A man asked the Holy Prophet (saws): "Sir, should I seek permission to enter my mother's house also?"

The Holy Prophet (saws) replied that he should. The man stated that there was nobody beside him to look after her, and asked whether it was necessary to get permission every time he wanted to go in. The Holy Prophet (saws) replied: "Yes; would you like that you should see your mother in a naked state?" According to a saying one should seek permission even when going to see one's own mother or sister. (Ibn Kathir) He has suggested that even when a person goes to visit one's wife in one's own house, he should announce his arrival by coughing, etc. It is related by his wife Zainab that `Abdullah bin Mas`ud would always announce his arrival by coughing, etc. and never liked that he should enter the house unannounced all of a sudden. (Ibn Jarir)

(4) The only exception to the general rule is that no permission is needed in case of an emergency, or a calamity like theft, fire, etc. One can go to help without permission in such cases.

(5) In the beginning when the system of seeking permission was introduced, people did not know the exact procedure to follow. Once a man came to the Prophet's (saws) house and shouted at the door, "Should I be in?" The Holy Prophet (saws) said to his maid servant, "Go and instruct him about the correct way. He should say: Assalam-o- `alaikum (peace be upon you). May I come in?" (Ibn Jarir, Abu Da'ud) Jabir bin `Abdullah says that once he went to the Holy Prophet's house in connection with certain liabilities of his father and knocked at the door. The Holy Prophet (saws) asked: "Who is it?" I replied, "It's me." The Holy Prophet thereupon repeated twice or thrice: "It's me, it's

me!" That is, how can one understand from this who you are? (Abu Da'ud)

A man went to see the Holy Prophet (saws) and got seated without the customary salutation. The Holy Prophet (saws) told him to go out and come in again after calling: Assalam-o-`alaikum (peace be upon you). (Abu Da'ud) Thus, the correct method of seeking permission was to disclose one's identity and then ask for permission. It is related that whenever Umar went to see the Holy Prophet (saws), he would say: "Assalam-o- alaikum ya Rasul-Allah, I am Umar. May I enter!" (Abu Da'ud) The Holy Prophet (saws) commanded that permission should be asked thrice at the most. If there is no reply even at the third call, one should come back. (Bukhari, Muslim, Abu D'ud) The same was his own practice.

Once he went to the house of a Companion, and sought permission twice after greeting with Assalam-o-`alaikum wa Rahmatullah (peace be upon you and mercy of Allah), but there was no response. After calling for the third time when he received no response, he turned back. Sa'd came out running from the house, and said, "O Messenger of Allah, I was hearing you all right, but I desired to have Allah's peace and mercy invoked upon me through your sacred tongue as often as possible. Therefore, I was replying to you in a low voice." (Abu Da'ud, Ahmad) The three calls as commanded above should not be made in quick succession, but at suitable intervals so as to allow sufficient time to the inmates to make the response in case they are not free to do so.

(6) The permission for entry should come from the master of the house himself, or from some other reliable inmate like a servant, or a responsible person, who gives permission on behalf of the master. One should not enter the house on the word of a mere child.

(7) Undue insistence for permission to enter, or to keep standing at the door obstinately even after refusal, is not permissible. If no entry is permitted even after three calls, or the master refuses to see you, one should go back.

Entry into an empty house is not allowed unless permitted by the master of the house. One may, for instance, have told a visitor, or sent him a message to wait in his room till his arrival. The mere fact that there is nobody in the house, or the call is not answered does not entitle anybody to enter without permission.

Nobody should mind if entry is refused. Everybody has a right to refuse to meet another person, or offer a plea if otherwise busy. The Command "Go back", according to the jurists, means going back in the literal sense, and moving away from the door. Nobody has any right to compel the other person for a meeting or to embarrass him by standing obstinately at his door.

"Houses which are not a dwelling place" are hotels, inns, guest houses, shops, staging bungalows, etc. which are generally open to all people.

Lightning Source UK Ltd.
Milton Keynes UK
UKHW010632171020
371758UK00001B/32